5

Our Valentine Book

By Jane Belk Moncure
Illustrated by
Mina Gow McLean

THE CHILD'S WORLD
ELGIN, ILLINOIS 60120

This is a book about how we celebrated Valentine's Day in our class. You will have more ideas in your class.

Library of Congress Cataloging in Publication Data

Moncure, Jane Belk.
  Our Valentine book.

  (Special Day book)
  SUMMARY: Describes various classroom activities in preparation for St. Valentine's Day.
  1. St. Valentine's Day—Juvenile literature.
2. Schools—Exercises and recreations—Juvenile literature. [1. St. Valentine's Day. 2. Holidays]
I. McLean, Mina. II. Title.
GT4925.M64   372.1'8'9   75-37678
ISBN 0-913778-32-X

Distributed by Childrens Press, 1224 West Van Buren Street, Chicago, Illinois 60607

"How do we know Valentine's Day is coming?" asked Miss Berry.

"We see valentines in stores," said Beth.

"We send valentines to friends," said Jeff.

"How can we send valentines to each other in our room?" asked the teacher.

"We can make our own post office," said John. Everyone agreed that was a good idea.

Miss Berry found a big box. She cut it so one side was open. John and Joe helped cut a big window in the box. Mary painted the words, "Post Office" across the front.

Then everyone decorated the post office with valentines.

Each person brought a shoe box from home for his own mail box.

"Let's see how many different ways you can decorate your mailboxes," said Miss Berry.

She put a large scrap box on the table. In it were pieces of colored paper, cloth, bits of ribbon, lacy paper doilies, and paper muffin cups.

Miss Berry cut a slot in each box; she stacked them on a shelf behind the post office.

Miss Berry made a sign for the post office. On one side was the word "open"; on the other side was the word "closed."

Whenever the post office was open, children could mail valentines. No one opened his own box, though. The boxes were to be opened on Valentine's Day.

One day Miss Berry said, "You are making such lovely valentines; let's think of some other ways to use them."

"We can put valentines together and make animals," said Amy. "Let's make an animal zoo and call it our valentine zoo."

The children used scraps of colored paper, paste, and tape. Miss Berry put the animal zoo on the bulletin board.

The next day, Miss Berry brought a little tree branch to school. "There are no leaves on this little tree," she said.

"We can put valentine leaves on it," said Ann. Soon children were busy decorating the valentine tree.

John hopped around the valentine tree singing his own song:
"Hop around the valentine tree.
Hop, hop, hop. One, two, three."

Scott was cutting out valentines. He cut one in half. "Look," he said. "I have made a valentine puzzle."

Miss Berry found some heavy paper. "Make each valentine puzzle a different color," she said. "See how many ways you can make valentine puzzles."

Here are some of Scott's puzzles from the valentine puzzle box. You can make others.

One day Amy and Melissa were working with some puppets. "We can make some valentine puppets," said Amy.

Miss Berry put the scrap box on a work table. Soon children were making all kinds of valentine puppets. Miss Berry stapled each puppet to a paper bag.

"Let's have a puppet show," said Melissa. "My puppet is the Queen of hearts."

"I am your dog, and it is my birthday," said Wendy.

Do you know what happened next? The puppets had a party.

"Miss Berry, can we have a valentine party on Valentine's Day?" asked Wendy and Melissa at the same time.

Everyone agreed that was a good idea. The class began making plans.

"We could invite our parents," said Jim.

"You can take the invitations home today," said Miss Berry. She wrote a message on the board. The children copied it on big pink valentines.

On Valentine's Day, Miss Berry brought a big bag to school.

"What is in the bag?" everyone asked.

"What do you think we forgot for our party?" she asked.

"Food!" said Joe.

"You guessed it," said Miss Berry. "I made the cupcakes, but you can decorate them."

Miss Berry gave each person a wooden spoon, some icing, and some tiny candy hearts. When the cupcakes were decorated, Miss Berry put them on a shelf.

The children worked together especially well all morning. Everyone knew the valentine party would be fun.

It was!

Tina's mother brought pink lemonade. Miss Berry gave everyone candy hearts. The cupcakes were sticky, but good. The children sang a valentine song and gave each parent a gift.

"Now we have a special surprise," said Miss Berry. "John, would you go to the door and invite our visitor inside?"

The next day, one group decorated paper napkins for the party. One group made place mats out of construction paper. Another group made paper valentine crowns for everyone.

"We have forgotten something," said Miss Berry.

On Valentine's Day, Miss Berry brought a big bag to school.

"What is in the bag?" everyone asked.

"What do you think we forgot for our party?" she asked.

"Food!" said Joe.

"You guessed it," said Miss Berry. "I made the cupcakes, but you can decorate them."

Miss Berry gave each person a wooden spoon, some icing, and some tiny candy hearts. When the cupcakes were decorated, Miss Berry put them on a shelf.

"Valentine's Day is a special day when we tell people we love them. You are giving each other valentines. What about your parents?"

"I know how to make a necklace with straws," said Tina. "We could make each mother and father a gift."

Miss Berry helped punch holes in valentines and cut straws into little pieces. Some children made necklaces out of these, using stiff string. Some made lapel pins. Others made valentine cards.

John said, "I would like to plan a surprise for everyone." He whispered something to Miss Berry.

John opened the door. There stood John's mother in her letter carrier uniform.

"A real letter carrier," everyone said.

"Since we have a post office, we will have a real letter carrier deliver our mail boxes on Valentine's Day," said Miss Berry. "This is John's mother, Letter Carrier Brown."

"Happy Valentine's Day," said Letter Carrier Brown as she gave each child a box full of valentines.